DOMESTIC EXTREMISM:
How Big Is the Threat?

Hal Marcovitz

ReferencePoint
Press

San Diego, CA

About the Author

Hal Marcovitz is a former newspaper reporter and columnist who lives in Chalfont, Pennsylvania. He has written more than two hundred books for young readers.

© 2022 ReferencePoint Press, Inc.
Printed in the United States

For more information, contact:
ReferencePoint Press, Inc.
PO Box 27779
San Diego, CA 92198
www.ReferencePointPress.com

LIBRARY OF CONGRESS CATALOGING-IN-PUBLICATION DATA

Names: Marcovitz, Hal., author.
Title: Domestic extremism: how big is the threat? / Hal Marcovitz.
Description: San Diego : ReferencePoint Press, 2022. | Includes
    bibliographical references and index.
Identifiers: LCCN 2021047021 (print) | ISBN
    9781678202361 (library binding) | ISBN 9781678202378 (ebook)
Subjects: LCSH: domestic extremism--United States--Juvenile literature. | Hate
    crimes—domestic terrorism--United States--Juvenile literature.

CONTENTS

**Important Events in the
History of Domestic Extremism**   4

Introduction   6
The Wolverine Watchmen

Chapter One   10
The Threat Posed by Domestic Extremism

Chapter Two   21
The Rise of Extremist Groups

Chapter Three   32
How Extremists Grow Their Ranks

Chapter Four   44
Countering Domestic Extremism

Source Notes   55
Organizations and Websites   58
For Further Research   60
Index   61
Picture Credits   64

IMPORTANT EVENTS IN THE HISTORY OF DOMESTIC EXTREMISM

1933
Adolf Hitler takes office as German chancellor, establishing the racist and anti-Semitic Nazi movement. Decades later, Nazi ideology is embraced by extremists in America.

1963
A bomb explodes at the 16th Street Baptist Church in Birmingham, Alabama, killing four young Black girls attending services. Eventually, three members of a Ku Klux Klan chapter are charged and convicted in the murders.

2012
President Barack Obama initiates the Deferred Action for Childhood Arrivals program, enraging extremists who oppose granting relief to undocumented immigrants.

| 1850 | 1950 | / | 2005 | 2010 | 2015 |

1865
At the end of the Civil War, the extremist group Ku Klux Klan forms in the South; the hooded and robed Klansmen embark on a decades-long mission to murder and abuse Black citizens.

1995
Extremist Timothy McVeigh ignites a bomb that destroys the Alfred P. Murrah Federal Building in Oklahoma City, Oklahoma, killing 168 people. McVeigh's death sentence is carried out in 2001.

2015
White nationalist Dylann Roof murders nine Black worshippers during a church service in Charleston, South Carolina; Roof is sentenced to death.

2016

In November Republican Donald Trump is elected US president. His anti-immigrant rhetoric is embraced by extremists. On December 4 a conspiracy theory known as "Pizzagate" prompts Edgar M. Welch to fire his rifle into a Washington, DC, pizza restaurant in the belief that he was freeing child prostitutes.

2019

Extremist Richard Holzer is arrested for plotting to blow up a synagogue in Pueblo, Colorado; he is convicted and sentenced to a prison term of nineteen years.

2020

In October thirteen members of the extremist group Wolverine Watchmen are arrested in a plot to kidnap Michigan governor Gretchen Whitmer. In November Democrat Joe Biden defeats Trump in the presidential election. Trump's false claims of voter fraud spark unrest by his extremist supporters.

2018

Facebook and other social media platforms begin banning posts by extremists after a group of Proud Boys assault peaceful demonstrators in New York City; Facebook establishes that incendiary posts by Proud Boys leaders sparked the assault.

2016   2017   2018   2019   2020

2021

On January 6, in response to Trump's claims that the presidency was stolen from him, hundreds of extremists break into the US Capitol in hopes of overturning the election results. Within the next several months, they are tracked down by the FBI and charged with participating in the riot. In June a team of White House national security advisers releases the *National Strategy for Countering Domestic Terrorism*, which outlines a $100 million plan to better monitor and investigate extremist groups in America.

2017

In May two men who came to the aid of seventeen-year-old Walia Mohamed on a train near Portland, Oregon, are fatally stabbed by extremist Jeremy Christian, who is harassing Mohamed. Christian is later convicted and sentenced to life in prison. In August hundreds of extremists participate in the Unite the Right rally in Charlottesville, Virginia; a counterprotester, Heather Heyer, is killed when extremist James Alex Fields Jr. drives his car into the crowd. Fields is later sentenced to life in prison.

The Wolverine Watchmen

In the fall of 2020, as the COVID-19 pandemic swept across America, many cities and towns remained in lockdown. Government leaders mandated that people avoid contact with one another as much as possible in order to minimize their likelihood of becoming infected with the deadly virus. Such "social distancing" rules included a ban on indoor dining in restaurants, the cancellation of many sporting events, the closure of shopping malls and gyms, the wearing of facial masks, and numerous other restrictions on daily life. Most Americans followed these rules, but a significant number urged defiance. In their view the government had no right to impose such restrictions on people's lives.

Among those who protested the COVID-19 restrictions were members of a group of extremists who called themselves the Wolverine Watchmen. Based in Michigan, leaders of the Wolverine Watchmen blamed the state's governor, Gretchen Whitmer, for mandating the strict COVID-19 rules. During the summer of 2020, leaders of the Wolverine Watchmen concocted a bizarre plot to kidnap the governor, stage a phony trial in which Whitmer would be accused of violating the rights of citizens by imposing the harsh COVID-19 guidelines, and ultimately execute Whitmer to punish her for her crimes.

Throughout the summer and early fall of 2020, according to the criminal complaint filed by prosecutors in the case, members of the Wolverine Watchmen accumulated weapons and ammunition and held training sessions in which they practiced assault tactics. Ultimately, they planned to kidnap Whitmer at her vacation home in rural Antrim County, Michigan. But the Federal Bureau of Investigation (FBI) learned of the group's plans. In October 2020 thirteen members of the Wolverine Watchmen were arrested and charged in the plot to kidnap and kill the governor.

Violent Tactics

The Wolverine Watchmen are one of many groups that have emerged in the twenty-first century that harbor so-called extremist views of American culture and the nation's system of government. Extremists may resort to incendiary rhetoric and violent tactics to create chaos and spread false accusations that are often based on bizarre and unproven conspiracy theories. Michigan attorney general Dana Nessel says:

> There has been a disturbing increase in anti-government rhetoric and the re-emergence of groups that embrace extremist ideologies. These groups often seek to recruit new members by seizing on a moment of civil unrest and using it to advance their agenda of self-reliance and armed resistance. This is more than just political disagreement or passionate advocacy, some of these groups' mission is simply to create chaos and inflict harm upon others.[1]

The Wolverine Watchmen was founded in 2019 by twenty-six-year-old Joe Morrison, who harbored a grudge against police after he was arrested for illegally carrying a concealed weapon.

In 2020 the FBI uncovered a plot by a group calling itself the Wolverine Watchmen to kidnap, try, and execute Michigan governor Gretchen Whitmer. The group was angry about the governor's COVID-19 mandates.

He created a Facebook page to air his grievances against police and soon found others in agreement with his views. By the fall of 2019, the Wolverine Watchmen had taken their movement beyond online chat and were meeting to voice their complaints. And by the spring of 2020, those complaints had focused on Whitmer and the restrictions she imposed on Michigan residents to slow the state's COVID-19 infection rate. On April 30, 2020, hundreds of demonstrators, including members of the Wolverine Watchmen, swarmed around the state capitol in Lansing, Michigan, to voice their complaints against the COVID-19 lockdown. The protest was largely peaceful: a single demonstrator, who police said was intoxicated, was arrested during the demonstration.

Sharing Prison Cells

Prosecutors allege that in the months following the April 30 protest at the Michigan capitol, Morrison and the others hatched the plot against Whitmer and came very close to carrying out their plans before the FBI was able to infiltrate the group and make the arrests. "Their anger at the Michigan governor was about her response to COVID-19, like shutting down gyms," says Seth Jones, a political science professor at Johns Hopkins University in Maryland. "And they really wanted to take action. What we see here is COVID-19 and the response to it, which has created anger against the government. COVID-19 is just adding to the long list of grievances that some small fringe groups have against the US government."[2] In August 2021 one of the participants, twenty-five-year-old Ty Garbin, pleaded guilty to participating in the conspiracy and was sentenced by a federal judge to more than six years in prison. By the fall of 2021, the remaining twelve members of the Wolverine Watchmen charged in the kidnap plot remained in jail awaiting trial.

"COVID-19 is just adding to the long list of grievances that some small fringe groups have against the US government."[2]

—Political science professor Seth Jones

The Wolverine Watchmen is just one of many such extremist groups that have emerged in recent years. Moreover, many individuals also harbor extremist viewpoints and have taken action on their own. They do this to call attention to their beliefs, cause chaos, and very often commit acts of violence under the misguided notions that their causes are justified and would find widespread acceptance by the American people. Very often, though, as in the case of the members of the Wolverine Watchmen, these extremists ultimately find themselves sharing prison cells.

CHAPTER ONE

The Threat Posed by Domestic Extremism

In May 2017 Walia Mohamed, a seventeen-year-old Black immigrant from the African nation of Somalia, was riding a commuter train in her adopted hometown of Portland, Oregon, when she suddenly heard hurtful comments shouted by a White man sitting nearby. At the time, she was wearing her hijab—a veil worn by many Muslim women. She was accompanied by a friend, Destinee Magnum, who is also Black but not a Muslim. According to court testimony, the man shouted at the two young women, "Muslims should die," "Go back to Saudi Arabia," and "Kill yourselves!"[3]

Three passengers aboard the train attempted to intervene. They approached the instigator and asked him to be quiet. An argument ensued. It grew into a scuffle. Suddenly, one of the men who came to the aid of the young women clutched his neck. Mohamed saw that he was bleeding. Mohamed says she realized then that the man who shouted the ethnic slurs had drawn a knife and used it to attack the three men who came to her aid. "I thought he was going to come after us and kill us too because of all the hateful things he was saying about Muslim people,"[4] Mohamed said during her testimony in court.

In fact, the instigator, Jeremy Christian, age thirty-eight, stabbed all three men. Two of them died: Taliesin Myrddin

Namkai-Meche, age twenty-three, and Rick Best, age fifty-three. The third man, Micah David-Cole Fletcher, age twenty-one, was wounded in the neck but survived.

Christian was arrested. In 2020 he was tried and convicted in a Portland courtroom in the fatal stabbings of Namkai-Meche and Best. A judge sentenced him to life imprisonment.

Christian did not testify at his trial, but witnesses portrayed him as an extremist—an individual who harbors racist views and is willing to use violence to advance his social and political visions. A month before the incident on the Portland train, witnesses at Christian's trial testified, they saw him in attendance at an extremist rally in a Portland park. Witnesses said they saw Christian carrying a baseball bat and heard him shout racist slurs. They also saw him thrust his hand into the air, making the Nazi salute. This gesture was common in 1930s and 1940s Germany under the regime known as the Third Reich, headed by leaders of the murderous and extremist Nazi Party. "We are talking about recreating the Third Reich," Christian wrote on his Facebook page. "You need unhindered and unhinged thugs for dirty work. A good thing we have the largest collection of them in the entire world."[5]

"Everywhere I go, I fear for my safety."[6]

—Walia Mohamed, who was targeted for verbal abuse by a White nationalist on a commuter train

As for Mohamed, she no longer wears her hijab in public. She fears that the sight of her wearing a hijab could spark similar outbursts from extremists and endanger her life. "Everywhere I go, I fear for my safety,"[6] she says.

Racist Principles

Christian's outburst illustrates the dangers posed by domestic extremism. In fact, the type of incident that led to the deaths of two men on the Portland train is becoming more and more common in American life. A 2021 analysis by the *Washington Post* found that since 2015, more than three hundred violent incidents that have occurred in America can be linked directly to extremist movements and ideologies. Moreover, those three hundred incidents have resulted in more than one hundred deaths. "What is most concerning is that the number of domestic terror plots and attacks are at the highest they have been in decades," says Seth Jones, a Johns Hopkins University political science professor. "It's so important for Americans to understand the gravity of the threat before it gets worse."[7]

According to the New York–based Anti-Defamation League—which fights anti-Semitism, extremism, and hate—extremism can be defined as follows:

> A concept used to describe religious, social or political belief systems that exist substantially outside of belief systems more broadly accepted in society. . . . Extreme ideologies often seek radical changes in the nature of government, religion or society. . . . Extremist movements exist outside of the mainstream because many of their views or tactics are objectionable.[8]

Many extremists have emerged out of the so-called alt-right movement. Short for "alternative-right," the title refers to an ideology at the utmost extreme end of conservative politics, frequently referred to as the right wing. In contrast, liberals—those who seek progressive change and acceptance of minorities—are said to occupy the left wing of American politics. Adherents to the alt-right ideology maintain White nationalist principles. They oppose civil rights for Black Americans. They harbor prejudices against Muslims, Latinos, and Asians. They are often vehemently anti-Semitic, meaning they dislike people of the Jewish faith. They maintain prejudices against members of the gay community. And they oppose immigration to America, particularly from countries in Central and South America, Africa, and the Islamic countries of Asia.

Attacks and Plots by Domestic Extremists, 2020

Violent far-right extremists engaged in far more terrorist plots and attacks in the United States in 2020 than other extremists. This is the finding of the Center for Strategic & International Studies (CSIS), which analyzed the US domestic terrorist threat between January 1 and August 31, 2020. CSIS identified sixty-one plots or attacks that took place during that period. Of those, two-thirds were committed by White supremacists and other like-minded extremists.

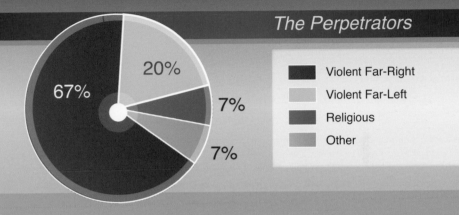

The Perpetrators

67% 20% 7% 7%

- Violent Far-Right
- Violent Far-Left
- Religious
- Other

Source: Seth G. Jones et al., "The War Comes Home: The Evolution of Domestic Terrorism in the United States," Center for Strategic & International Studies, October 22, 2020. www.csis.org.

Domestic Terrorism

But extremists often do more than just spout hateful rhetoric toward members of racial and ethnic groups they despise. In many cases extremists commit acts of what the FBI has characterized as "domestic terrorism," meaning extremists carry out violent acts aimed at people they perceive as their enemies. According to a 2021 report by the FBI, from 2015 to 2019 a total of 846 individuals in America were charged with committing acts of domestic terrorism. The report describes a typical case:

> In November 2019, Richard Holzer was arrested for plotting to blow up the Temple Emanuel Synagogue in Pueblo, Colorado, conduct that constituted an act of domestic terrorism. Holzer told undercover FBI agents he wanted the

bombing to send a message to Jewish people that they must leave his town, "otherwise people will die." He pleaded guilty to federal hate crime and explosives charges, and in February 2021 he was sentenced to over 19 years in prison, followed by 15 years of supervised release.[9]

The FBI was able to arrest Holzer before he carried out his plans to blow up the synagogue and murder whoever may have been inside the temple at the time. In other cases, though, the FBI as well as other law enforcement agencies have been unable to gain intelligence on the plans of domestic extremists—and lives have been lost. In 1995 extremist Timothy McVeigh detonated a bomb outside the Alfred P. Murrah Federal Building in Oklahoma City, Oklahoma. The blast destroyed much of the building, killing 168 people inside. McVeigh was arrested and sentenced to death. McVeigh was a decorated veteran of the 1991 Persian Gulf War, in which the American military was deployed to defend the Middle East nation of Kuwait against an invasion by Iraq, a neigh-

Domestic extremism is not limited to hateful rhetoric. In 1995 antigovernment extremist Timothy McVeigh detonated a bomb outside the federal building in Oklahoma City. The blast destroyed much of the building (pictured) and killed 168 people inside.

boring state. And yet McVeigh had become increasingly convinced that the federal government aimed to deny rights to Americans—particularly the US Constitution's provision guaranteeing the right to own guns. His anger against the government led him to plant the bomb at the Murrah Building. In 2001 the federal government carried out the death sentence against McVeigh.

"Dylann Roof murdered African Americans at their church, during their Bible-study and worship. They had welcomed him. He slaughtered them."[10]

—Three-judge panel, 4th US Circuit Court of Appeals

Domestic terrorism again surfaced in 2015. That year White nationalist Dylann Roof made his way into Mother Emanuel AME Church in Charleston, South Carolina. Services at the church are attended by a largely Black congregation. Roof drew a gun, fired indiscriminately, and murdered nine people. In 2016 a jury found him guilty. By the fall of 2021, Roof remained in a federal prison awaiting the execution of his sentence—the death penalty.

Following his conviction, Roof's attorneys filed legal appeals, seeking to spare their client the death penalty, but judges have consistently dismissed the appeals. In August 2021 a panel of three judges, asked to reconsider the sentence, turned down his latest appeal, writing, "Dylann Roof murdered African Americans at their church, during their Bible-study and worship. They had welcomed him. He slaughtered them. He did so with the express intent of terrorizing not just his immediate victims at the historically important Mother Emanuel Church, but as many similar people as would hear of the mass murder."[10]

And in August 2017 hundreds of extremists participated in the so-called Unite the Right rally in Charlottesville, Virginia. While members of extremist groups paraded, shouting racist and anti-Semitic rhetoric, a few dozen counterprotesters gathered nearby to demonstrate against extremism. One of the extremists, James Alex Fields Jr., responded to the counterprotest by driving his vehicle into the crowd, killing a woman named Heather Heyer. Fields was convicted in the murder of Heyer and sentenced to life in prison.

Extremism in the Police and Military

Many Americans find it truly shocking when they learn that extremist violence has erupted on a commuter train, in a public park, in a federal office building, or during Sunday morning church services. But in recent years evidence has also come to light suggesting that extremist views have become popular among members of the US military as well as many American police departments. This evidence is included in a 2021 report by the Center for Strategic and International Studies (CSIS), a Washington, DC–based organization that studies national security threats. The CSIS report found that many current and former members of the military and American police departments have been drawn into extremist movements. The report cited the case of Jarrett William Smith, a twenty-four-year-old US Army infantry soldier stationed at Fort Riley in Kansas, who used his Facebook page in 2019 to post instructions on how to make homemade bombs.

Smith expressed admiration for Nazism on his Facebook page and said he desired to spark a war between the races, pitting Blacks against Whites—with the ultimate goal of driving Black people out of American society. He suggested that a first step in sparking the race war would be to send bombs to news organizations, particularly the cable news network CNN.

One of Smith's followers on Facebook was Timothy Wilson, a US Navy veteran who had espoused his hatred for Blacks, Jews, and immigrants. A resident of the Kansas City, Missouri, suburb of Belton, Wilson planned to use Smith's techniques for bomb making to blow up a local hospital treating COVID-19 patients. Other targets were believed to be a synagogue, a mosque, and a school attended largely by Black students. In 2020 FBI agents learned of the plot. When they moved in to arrest Wilson, he took his own life. As for Smith, he was arrested and sentenced to a federal prison term of thirty months. In sentencing Smith, US district judge Daniel Crabtree said, "His planned actions, if executed, would have endangered countless members of the public."[11]

Domestic extremists who resort to violence to achieve their aims are not unique to far-right groups. Extremists have also emerged from the left wing of American politics. Many have roots in the environmental movement, often resorting to violence against institutions they believe are responsible for polluting the environment or contributing to climate change. Law enforcement officials refer to such extremists as "eco-terrorists."

In December 2020 two Washington State women, twenty-three-year-old Ellen Brennan Reiche and twenty-seven-year-old Samantha Frances Brooks, were charged with tampering with train tracks near the Canadian border in an attempt to force a train derailment. Although their plan was foiled at the last minute—a security camera caught them in the act and police arrived while they were still at the scene—it could have led to the deaths and injuries of passengers aboard a train. Federal prosecutors believe the women carried out the plan to protest the extension of an oil pipeline from Canada into the United States. The burning of oil, a fossil fuel, is a primary cause of climate change. Says Steven Beda, a history professor at the University of Oregon, "This is a debate that is hardly unique to the environmental movement . . . any major social movement in world history has had this debate about whether they should go through the political and legal systems to get the change they want, or whether they should engage in more radical forms of activism."

Brooks pleaded guilty in July 2021 and by the fall of 2021 was awaiting sentencing. By the fall of 2021, Reiche had yet to come to trial.

Quoted in Hilary Beaumont, "The Activists Sabotaging Railways in Solidarity with Indigenous People," *The Guardian*, July 29, 2021. www.theguardian.com.

Moreover, across the country, city mayors and police superintendents have learned that the ranks of their police departments often include officers who harbor extremist views. In 2021 seventy-two police officers in Philadelphia, Pennsylvania, received temporary suspensions when department officials discovered racist posts by those officers on their Facebook pages. Ultimately, thirteen of those officers were fired.

Reacting to Societal Change

Whether extremists who identify with the alt-right movement can be found in the military, police departments, or other corners of American society, one trait that is common among most extremists is their fear of change. And in American society, change has often resulted in the expansion of rights guaranteed for Blacks, Latinos, gay Americans, and others whom domestic extremists are known to detest.

Extremists see these changes occurring around them in society and they feel marginalized and powerless to alter the direction of the culture in which they live. They see American culture evolving around them and find themselves harboring fears about what the future may hold. Says Laura Ingraham, a Fox News commentator who is popular among alt-right extremists, "The America we know and love doesn't exist anymore. . . . Massive demographic changes have been foisted on the American people, and they are changes that none of us ever voted for and most of us don't like."[12]

Certainly, many people welcome change. Others just learn to live with it. But domestic extremists are largely unwilling to accept change. They find solace and acceptance in the extremist

White nationalists march at the University of Virginia the night before the 2017 Unite the Right rally in Charlottesville. At the rally, an extremist drove his car into a crowd of counter-protesters, killing one woman.

The Extremist Response to Black Lives Matter

The Black Lives Matter (BLM) movement reached a crescendo in American society during the summer of 2020 after the death of George Floyd. Floyd, who was arrested on a minor charge, was murdered by a police officer in Minneapolis, Minnesota. During the tumultuous months that followed, thousands of protesters filled American streets to demonstrate against police abuse of Black citizens.

The protesters were often met by extremists who lashed out against them with violence. Reports a *Washington Post* analysis of the extremist response to the BLM movement, "Perpetrators beat BLM activists in the streets and attacked them with mace, knives, guns or explosives, records show. Right-wing extremists used their vehicles as weapons against activists, plowing into crowds of racial justice demonstrators."

Moreover, extremists vandalized many Black-owned businesses, including some that were set on fire. Darnesha Weary, co-owner of Black Coffee Northwest and a BLM coordinator in Shoreline, Washington, says her shop was vandalized with racist graffiti. She says, "No one should feel like they have the audacity to go try and burn someone's building. And just because they're mad."

Quoted in Robert O'Harrow Jr. et al., "The Rise of Domestic Terrorism Is Fueled Mostly by Far-Right Extremists, Analysis Shows," *Philadelphia Inquirer*, April 12, 2021. www.inquirer.com.

movements where they find others who agree with their worldviews. Says Chris Bosley, a former senior adviser to the US Office of National Intelligence, an agency that assesses threats to American security:

> As people search for answers to their frustrations, and legitimate channels seem inadequate or unable to rectify or even acknowledge their grievances, voices that present simplistic answers to complex questions, paint legitimate grievances and innate fears of sociocultural change as assaults on an entire social group or way of life, and misplace blame for the hardships they face can be appealing. When people feel like their identity is under assault, millions of years of inherited evolutionary biology kick in, and our brains respond in the same way that they would to physical threats—literally dehumanizing the assailants and removing cognitive inhibitions to using violence in defense of the group.[13]

As Bosley suggests, that fear of change can prompt extremists to embrace solutions that include committing violence or other illegal acts to oppose changes in the society in which they live. According to Christian Picciolini, a former member of the extremist movement:

Extremism, regardless of whether it's motivated by a political, religious, or social doctrine, flourishes when a critical mass of people believe their lives are becoming meaningless, displaced, or disempowered. Extremists feast on frenzy and polarization during times of crisis. Fear is primary sustenance for extremism to thrive, and its survival rests on the ability to foment the chaotic conditions that keeps us broken and afraid.[14]

Although extremists may not welcome change, there is no question that societal change is a common element of life in America. And while it is true that change often does not come quickly, it is also certainly true that American society is a lot different than it was generations ago. Moreover, in the future American society is likely to be vastly different from what people see around them today. It means that extremism is not only a threat to peace in today's society, it could very well continue to be a threat to Americans in the years to come as their society continues to change. And as American society inevitably does change and becomes more and more welcoming of Blacks, Latinos, and other minority communities, it is likely that there will continue to exist a culture that includes American citizens who simply cannot accept change and are often likely to resort to violence in the mistaken belief that their tactics could somehow stall that change.

"Extremism, regardless of whether it's motivated by a political, religious, or social doctrine, flourishes when a critical mass of people believe their lives are becoming meaningless, displaced, or disempowered."[14]

—Former extremist leader Christian Picciolini

20

CHAPTER TWO

The Rise of Extremist Groups

Christian Picciolini discovered the extremist movement in 1987 at age fourteen. Growing up in the Chicago suburb of Blue Island, Illinois, Picciolini and a friend were standing in an alley one afternoon sharing a marijuana cigarette when a man suddenly drove up in a flashy sports car. He slammed on the brakes, got out of the car, and confronted the two teens. "He pulled the joint from my mouth, looked me in the eyes, and he said, 'That's what the communists and the Jews want you to do, to keep you docile,'"[15] Picciolini recalls.

Picciolini says he was confused by the man's comment. He did not know anything about the economic principle of communism—which was embraced by the repressive regime in the former Soviet Union—nor did he know any people of the Jewish faith. Still, it was a time in his life when he felt rebellious against authority and often felt confused and aimless. He was unsure of how he planned to spend the rest of his life. "He saw that I was lonely, and I was certainly doing something that put me on the fringes already—smoking pot in an alley. He knew that I was searching for three very important things: a sense of identity, a community and a purpose. . . . It was the first time in my young life that I felt somebody had actually paid attention to me, and empowered me in some way,"[16] Picciolini says.

It turned out that the man who drove up in the alley that day was Clark Martell, leader of a local extremist group known as the Chicago Area Skinheads, or CASH. (*Skinhead* is a nickname that has been adopted by many extremists who prefer to shave their scalps bare.) Martell invited Picciolini to attend a CASH rally scheduled for a few days later. Picciolini rode his bicycle to the rally. He heard the CASH leaders spout racist and anti-Semitic rhetoric. He attended other rallies, finding himself drawn into the movement. He joined CASH and soon earned a place as Martell's top lieutenant.

Two years after meeting Martell in the alley and joining CASH, Picciolini found himself leading the extremist group. Martell had been arrested for a violent assault on a former CASH member and sentenced to a prison term of eleven years. At age sixteen, Picciolini took over the leadership of CASH and soon proved himself to be a skilled organizer and tactician in the Chicago area extremist community. He engineered a merger between CASH and a similar group known as Hammerskin Nation. He also founded a punk rock band known as White American Youth, which produced songs with racist lyrics. The band was very much in demand to provide entertainment at extremist rallies in America as well as Europe.

Picciolini was often an enthusiastic participant when it came to committing acts of violence. He recalls one occasion in which he walked into a fast-food restaurant with some skinhead friends. They saw a group of Black youths in the restaurant. Picciolini shouted at the Black teens, ordering them to leave the restaurant. The frightened teens immediately left, but Picciolini and his friends gave chase. They caught up with the teens outside the restaurant and started throwing punches. Picciolini cornered one of the youths. "I remember beating him, kicking him, punching him until his face was swollen," he says. "And I remember him on the ground looking up at me through swollen eyes as I was kicking him. His eyes were pleading with mine to stay alive."[17]

Growing Into a National Movement

Picciolini's experience illustrates how young extremists can easily be drawn into the movement by others, such as Martell, who find a way to empower them and encourage extremist behavior among their young recruits. Many activists form extremist associations that often start out as neighborhood groups composed of a few friends, but some of these groups have eventually grown into national movements. Today groups such as the Proud Boys, Oath Keepers, and Boogaloo Bois include chapters in many major cities as well as rural communities.

Very often, residents are shocked to learn that such groups exist in their neighborhoods. In May 2021, for example, a group of Jewish residents and others held a rally in Boca Raton, Florida, to show their support for the nation of Israel. The rally was interrupted by horns blaring from a caravan of vehicles that drove past the event. Many of the vehicles displayed signs reading "Hitler was Right," while drivers and their passengers shouted

Extremist groups including the Proud Boys (pictured at a 2020 rally in Portland, Oregon) have become adept at recruiting followers. Many of these groups have chapters in cities and rural communities.

anti-Semitic messages toward the rally attendees. (The signs referred to the doctrine espoused by German chancellor Adolf Hitler, under whose orders some 6 million European Jews were murdered in concentration camps in the 1930s and 1940s.) Says Efrem Goldberg, a Boca Raton rabbi, "We rally for peace and this van filled with hate, calls for genocide and threats, kept circling. Hard to believe in the heart of Boca Raton if [I] didn't see it myself."[18]

The counterrally was organized by Jovanni Valle, founder of an extremist group known as the Goyim Defense League, or GDL. (The term *goyim* is a derogatory expression found in the Yiddish and Hebrew languages for non-Jewish people.) According to the Anti-Defamation League, "GDL attracts a range of anti-Semites and White supremacists who are motivated and united by their hatred of Jews. The most zealous GDL actors are in California, Colorado, Florida and New York. They work alone, in small local cliques and occasionally travel across the country to work together in larger teams."[19]

Arrival of the Ku Klux Klan

Although extremist groups like the GDL, Proud Boys, and Hammerskin Nation have been established in recent years, extremist groups are not new to American society. Following the end of the Civil War in 1865, the US Congress passed the Thirteenth Amendment to the Constitution, outlawing slavery. But bitterness and hostility toward the freed slaves persisted in the South. In the months following the defeat of the South, the extremist group Ku Klux Klan was established by veterans of the Confederate army. The Klan remained an underground organization for decades; its members wore white robes and hoods as they rode the back trails of the South, kidnapping and lynching Black citizens. In the decades following the end of the Civil War, historians have esti-

Women and Extremism

Many male extremists view women with some level of contempt, or misogyny. They do not view women as equals, but that has not stopped women from joining extremist movements. Among them are Tara LaRosa, who enjoyed a career as a star of women's Mixed Martial Arts (MMA) competitions. She retired from the MMA circuit in 2015. Since leaving the sport, she has become a familiar figure at many extremist rallies.

Scholars who have looked into the appeal that extremist groups hold for women note that the draw for women is not all that different from men. "The rapid growth in the number of female far-right supporters demonstrates that women are not immune to racist mindsets and more broadly extremist ideologies, which hold contempt for human nature," write Julia Ebner and Jacob Davey, researchers for the Washington, DC, public policy group Institute for Strategic Dialogue.

And while men in these movements might not value their female peers, it is the women—especially the social media influencers—who have helped far-right ideologies find mainstream acceptance. The researchers note: "The widespread presence of women in far-right movements has played a significant role in the mainstreaming and normalization of white nationalist, anti-migration and anti-Muslim views."

Julia Ebner and Jacob Davey, "How Women Advance the Internationalization of the Far-Right," *Perspectives on the Future of Women, Gender & Violent Extremism*, February 1, 2019, p. 32. https://extremism.gwu.edu.

mated that some two thousand Black citizens in the South lost their lives in lynchings committed by Ku Klux Klan members and other extremists.

In the first decades of the twentieth century, the Klan often emerged from the underground, its members parading publicly and in many cases eschewing their robes and hoods. They no longer felt the need to hide their memberships in the organization. According to the Equal Justice Initiative, an Alabama-based civil rights group, as many as 4 million citizens of the southern states held memberships in Ku Klux Klan chapters during the 1920s.

In the twenty-first century, law enforcement officials believe there are still active chapters of the Ku Klux Klan. Those chapters are hardly alone now in maintaining extremist views and providing platforms for extremists to share their beliefs, fears, and often violent plans to target Blacks, Latinos, and others.

Extremist Attitudes Toward Immigrants and Women

While the Ku Klux Klan has been in existence for more than a century, other extremist groups are relatively new. The Southern Poverty Law Center (SPLC), an Alabama-based organization that tracks extremist activity in America, says hundreds of extremist groups have been established in the past two decades. Among them are the Oath Keepers, which was founded in 2009 as a reaction to the 2008 election of Barack Obama as the nation's first Black president.

Obama further angered members of the Oath Keepers and other extremist groups when he signed an order in 2012 creating a program known as Deferred Action for Childhood Arrivals. The program ended the federal government's policy of deporting children who, with their parents, entered the United States illegally. "Obama's declaration of intent to rule by decree and grant 'amnesty' to millions of illegal aliens is an impeachable offense, and Obama should be impeached and removed from office,"[20] Oath Keepers founder Stewart Rhodes declared in 2014.

Hostility toward Barack Obama, the nation's first Black president, spilled over into hostility toward his policies. The DACA program, which protects children brought to the United States illegally by their parents, was the object of extremist ire.

Obama won reelection in 2012 and served until January 2017. (Under law, presidents are limited to no more than two terms in office.) In the spring of 2016, Republican Donald Trump emerged as the frontrunner to win his party's nomination for the presidential election. Trump's rhetoric during the campaign clearly appealed to many extremists. He opposed immigration from Mexico and Central American countries, calling for the construction of a wall along the US border with Mexico. And prior to commencing his campaign for the presidency, Trump charged—falsely—that Obama was not born in the United States and therefore, under law, was unqualified to be president. The charge clearly appealed to the White supremacists in the extremist movement, who were always loath to accept Obama as a legitimate president. By the summer of 2016, Trump had the Republican nomination wrapped up.

He faced Democrat Hillary Clinton in the fall campaign. A former First Lady and senator from New York State, Clinton served as secretary of state in the Obama administration.

During the campaign of 2016, the Oath Keepers, Proud Boys, and other extremist groups focused their hatred squarely toward Clinton. Rhodes predicted that Clinton would find a way to confiscate firearms from American gun owners. He wrote, "Imagine [Hillary Clinton] is sworn in as president. . . . After a conveniently timed 'domestic terrorism' incident (just a coincidence, of course) . . . she promptly crams a United Nations mandated total ban on the private possession of firearms."[21] Rhodes further predicted that Clinton would establish secret military detention sites across the country, where she would imprison citizens who defied her orders to surrender their firearms. In fact, at no time during the campaign did Clinton call for the confiscation of privately held firearms.

If elected, Clinton would have been the first woman to hold the office of president in America. This clearly troubled many extremists, who believe women should be subservient to men. Members of the Proud Boys are, for example, virtually all males. And among their stated principles are to "venerate the housewife,"[22] which means they do not support women who wish to seek professional careers. Rather, the Proud Boys prefer women remain at home, cooking suppers, cleaning the house, and minding the children. In a 2018 interview, Proud Boys founder Gavin McInnes told a journalist:

> I would say that feminism was done in maybe 1979. And since then, it's just been women inventing problems and lying to create a world where feminists are needed. Like saying one in four women will be sexually assaulted or raped in college—or saying that women earn less than men and there's a wage gap. Like just blatant lies to justify their existence.
>
> Women tend to choose jobs that are less strenuous, less risky, they tend to want to go home for their daughter's piano recital rather than stay at the office all night, and that costs them promotions down the line.[23]

Trump's Appeal to Extremists

Trump was often known to display a contempt for women—a fact that further enhanced his popularity among extremists. In the 2016 campaign for the presidency, a videotaped interview with a reporter from the TV show *Access Hollywood* surfaced in which Trump boasted about sexually assaulting women. And after winning the Republican nomination for president in the summer of 2016, Trump named Steve Bannon as his campaign manager. At the time, Bannon was the editor of Breitbart News, a website known for spreading extremist views. Among the stories published

"Women tend to choose jobs that are less strenuous, less risky, they tend to want to go home for their daughter's piano recital rather than stay at the office all night, and that costs them promotions down the line."[23]

—Proud Boys founder Gavin McInnes

Sovereign Citizens

Extremism in American society is not limited to White nationalists. In July 2021 police encountered a group of eleven armed Black men, dressed in military-style gear, along a highway near the town of Wakefield, Massachusetts. After a nine-hour standoff, the men surrendered to police. "You can imagine 11 armed individuals standing with long guns slung on an interstate highway at 2 in the morning certainly raises concerns," says Christopher Mason, a colonel with the Massachusetts State Police.

After taking the men into custody, police learned they were members of a group calling itself Rise of the Moors. According to the Montgomery, Alabama–based Southern Poverty Law Center, Rise of the Moors can be characterized as a "sovereign citizens" group, meaning its members have renounced their US citizenship and do not believe domestic laws apply to them.

People of Moorish ancestry trace their roots to the African nation of Morocco. Today the country is something of a tourist destination; the Moroccan government invites visitors from the West to explore the country's sandy beaches and the exotic cities of Tangier and Casablanca. As for the members of Rise of the Moors, in the fall of 2021 the eleven members remained in custody, awaiting trial for their roles in the armed standoff.

Quoted in Associated Press, "11 Held After Armed Standoff Closes Part of I-95 in Massachusetts," *Philadelphia Inquirer*, July 4, 2021, p. A2.

on Bannon's website was the phony allegation that birth control pills rob women of their beauty.

Breitbart's (and Bannon's) leanings could be seen in other stories. One story ran under the headline "Hoist It High and Proud: The Confederate Flag Proclaims a Glorious Heritage." That story advocated for the preservation of the Confederate "stars and bars" flag as an important symbol of American culture. Black Americans and many others regard the Confederate flag as a symbol of racism and treason. In addition, Breitbart published a criticism of Bill Kristol, a well-known political pundit, calling him a "renegade Jew"[24] for opposing Trump's candidacy for the presidency. All of these factors made Trump particularly popular among extremists and helped ignite the movement, drawing in new members.

In the November 2016 election, Trump won a narrow victory over Clinton. Throughout the next four years of his presidency,

Trump continued to win approval from extremists. For example, after the 2017 rally in Charlottesville, Virginia, which took the life of counterprotester Heather Heyer, Trump refused to denounce the rally or its extremist messages. "[There] were very fine people on both sides,"[25] Trump insisted after the rally.

Siege on the US Capitol

Trump's popularity among domestic extremists is regarded as largely responsible for the January 6, 2021, siege on the US Capitol. When numerous courts and the US Congress refused to overturn the results of the 2020 presidential election, finding no fraud in the casting of millions of votes, Trump called on his followers to demonstrate at the Capitol. "We fight like hell," Trump told thousands of his followers gathered for a rally near the Capitol in Washington, DC, the morning of January 6. "And if you don't fight like hell, you're not going to have a country anymore."[26]

Rioters force their way into the Capitol building on January 6, 2021. Among the crowd were members of various extremist groups who were reacting to Donald Trump's false claim that fraud resulted in a stolen election victory.

Many members of extremist groups marched among the members of the crowd who made their way to the Capitol that morning. When the crowd arrived at the Capitol, demonstrators forced their way into the building, soon overrunning police officers standing guard. They ransacked and looted offices, forcing members of Congress and staff members to flee for their lives. Hours later, reinforcements from the Metropolitan Police Department in Washington, DC, as well as the National Guard arrived to break up the siege. Four demonstrators and one police officer died during the melee. In the months following the siege, the FBI arrested more than six hundred participants in the assault, charging them with crimes stemming from the day's events. By the fall of 2021, more than fifty of the rioters had pleaded guilty, with some receiving jail sentences.

> "We fight like hell. And if you don't fight like hell, you're not going to have a country anymore."[26]
>
> —Former president Donald Trump

According to the SPLC, among the extremist groups whose members participated in the siege were the Proud Boys, Boogaloo Bois, and Oath Keepers. Other less well-known groups included No White Guilt, the Three Percenters, and Rise Above Nation. "It runs the whole gamut of different groups, from soup to nuts, A to Z . . . everything's on the table in terms of extremist groups,"[27] says Michael Sherwin, the acting US attorney for Washington, DC.

The Capitol siege illustrates that domestic extremism poses a very real threat to the American people and to the nation's democratic institutions. In fact, on January 6, 2021, many members of extremist groups believed their movement had grown so strong that they would actually be able to take over the government of the United States and overturn the results of a national election. Ultimately, they were proved wrong.

CHAPTER THREE

How Extremists Grow Their Ranks

Nextdoor is a social media platform that offers neighbors opportunities to share information and solve problems. Looking for a plumber? Post the request on Nextdoor, and chances are someone in the neighborhood can recommend one. When do sign-ups begin for Little League? Someone on Nextdoor surely knows the answer. Is your cat missing? Post a photo of your pet on Nextdoor and ask neighbors to keep an eye out. Chances are good a neighbor will spot the cat.

Given the type of posts that are commonly found on Nextdoor, in September 2020 a resident of the Phoenix, Arizona, neighborhood of Tramonto was shocked when he opened his Nextdoor app and saw a post inviting local residents to join a Proud Boys chapter. "[The poster] did say he's already got seven people who did sign up in our area for the Proud Boys,"[28] the Tramonto resident told a reporter.

The Tramonto man declined to give his name to the reporter, and it is easy to see why. When the man posted a protest on Nextdoor, suggesting the platform was no place to recruit members for a White nationalist extremist group, the Proud Boys recruiter responded with a series of threatening posts. "They were threatening to come and interfere with my life," the Tramonto man said. "Obviously, I have a family and kids."[29] He feared that permitting the media to publish his name would lead to more intimidation and perhaps retribution by the Proud Boys.

Conspiracy Theories

The use of social media platforms like Nextdoor illustrates how extremist groups have made use of the internet to grow their ranks. But extremists use social media for much more than just posting dates and times for the next Proud Boys rally. Rather, extremists routinely use social media to post baseless and bizarre conspiracy theories in the hopes their lies will be accepted as the truth, inciting people to join their movement.

The most widely read author of conspiracy theories on the internet is a mysterious extremist who posts under the name QAnon—often referred to simply as "Q." Among the phony pronouncements by QAnon are that the US government is dominated by Satan worshippers, including men and women who sexually abuse children. Also, QAnon insists that leaders of the military are plotting to take over the federal government.

QAnon is not the sole source of conspiracy theories that have prompted extremists to commit unlawful acts. And unlike QAnon, many of these other conspiracy theory spreaders are not anonymous. For example, Texas-based radio host Alex Jones maintains the InfoWars website, on which he regularly posts conspiracy theories. Among his theories are the baseless allegation that the US Air Force is able to control the weather, specifically suggesting that a torrential downpour caused by military aircraft over Texas in 2013 killed more than thirty people. Another theory Jones has posted suggests that the US military developed a gas that when inhaled causes its victims to turn gay. Says Jones, "The reason there's so many gay people now is because it's a chemical warfare operation, and I have the government documents where they said they're going to encourage homosexuality with chemicals so that people don't have children."[30]

QAnon supporters rally for Donald Trump's reelection in 2020. Extremists, including groups such as QAnon, use social media to post baseless and bizarre conspiracy theories in the hopes their lies will be accepted as truth and inspire new followers.

In 2016 Jones promoted a conspiracy theory known as "Pizzagate," suggesting that a popular pizza restaurant in Washington, DC, was in fact the headquarters of a child prostitute trafficking ring headed by leaders of the federal government. On December 4 Jones's pronouncement prompted twenty-eight-year-old Edgar M. Welch of Salisbury, North Carolina, to burst into the restaurant and fire a military-style rifle, believing he was on a mission to save the children. No one was injured in the incident. As for Welch, he served a prison term of three years. Says the SPLC, "After an FBI complaint showed that Welch had been watching an InfoWars 'documentary' promoting the conspiracy theory, Jones scrubbed his site of most of its Pizzagate content in an apparent effort to distance himself from the fallout of this particularly toxic lie."[31]

Conspiracy Theories on Social Media

Conspiracy theories concocted by Jones, QAnon, and others are generally not reported by the mainstream press. The newspapers do not report such accusations, nor are they featured on network or cable news broadcasts. Rather, it is likely that most people who encounter these bizarre tales do so on social media. In 2020 the UK-based Institute for Strategic Dialogue, which tracks extremist activity around the world, identified 109 Facebook groups known to circulate QAnon conspiracy theories. The group calculated the membership in those Facebook groups at more than 1.1 million people. Likewise, in early 2021 administrators of the Twitter social media platform disclosed that some seventy thousand Twitter accounts regularly circulated QAnon conspiracy theories.

And while conspiracy theories can be found circulating on social media virtually every day, these bizarre stories find their most traction during times of national crises. During the protests against racial injustice that dominated American society in 2020, extremist groups were quick to circulate racist conspiracy theories in the hopes of generating fear among White social media subscribers that Black people intended to do them harm. In July 2020 an extremist group that identified itself as California Patriots Pro Law & Order created a post on its Facebook page charging that the Black protesters who took to the streets to demonstrate against police abuse had actually been paid to cause trouble. Moreover, the group insisted on its Facebook page that the death of George Floyd, which sparked the national demonstrations against police abuse, had been staged and that Floyd did not die in the incident.

During the protests against police abuse, the billionaire George Soros often found himself under attack on social media platforms. Soros has donated billions of dollars to progressive causes, including many that work toward ensuring civil rights for

Extremist groups have made many outrageous claims. One group contends that the death of George Floyd, which sparked nationwide protests against police abuse, was staged and that Floyd did not die in the incident.

Black Americans and other members of minority groups. During the protests against police abuse, Soros was accused on social media of paying for buses that transported Black protesters from neighborhood to neighborhood. And some social media posts suggested that Soros paid for bricks that were handed to Black protesters, who were instructed to hurl them through the windows of stores that lined the streets along the protest routes.

On June 20, 2020, as anti–police abuse protests swept through a number of cities, a Twitter account created under the name "SearchWarrant" posted a photo of Soros and this fictional comment attributed to the billionaire: "I'm going to bring down the United States by funding Black Hate groups. We'll put them into a mental trap and make them blame White people. The Black community is the easiest to manipulate."[32]

Soros is a Jewish immigrant from Hungary. Many of the attacks against him have been tinged with anti-Semitic rhetoric. In many of the posts on Twitter, Facebook, and other social media platforms, Soros was accused of financing the protests against police abuse. The Anti-Defamation League calculated that shortly after the death of Floyd on May 25, 2020, some five hundred thousand posts a day surfaced on Twitter accusing Soros of orchestrating the protests. Author Talia Lavin, who has studied the extremist movement, says:

"The Internet has without question made it easier for conspiracy theorists to connect with one another, to build power through organizing and the steady rollout of ever-slicker propaganda."[33]

—Author Talia Lavin

The Internet has without question made it easier for conspiracy theorists to connect with one another, to build power through organizing and the steady rollout of ever-slicker propaganda. And anti-Semitic rhetoric has bloomed like a bog flower in the swampier parts of YouTube, Twitter, and Facebook. . . . What makes white supremacist worldviews more comprehensive and textured than a simple animus [hostility] against nonwhites is their addition of the Jew, the nefarious foe who seeks to upend the natural racial order. . . . Not all white supremacist ideologies center on anti-Semitic conspiracy—but for many of the ideologues of organized racism, the Jew is rhetorically indispensable as he is evil.[33]

Believing Conspiracy Theories

When conspiracy theories are circulated so widely on social media and elsewhere on the internet, there is no question that they gain traction, and many people become convinced they are true. Indeed, Welch became convinced that a pizza restaurant was serving as the headquarters of a child sex ring and took it upon himself to free the victims of the ring—only there was no child sex ring or victims, and Welch ended up in jail. Other conspiracy theories circulated by extremists have similarly prompted believers to take action.

Seventeen-year-old Kyle Rittenhouse of Antioch, Illinois, was a close follower of a Facebook group created by an extremist group known as the Kenosha Guard, headquartered in nearby Kenosha, Wisconsin. In August 2020 protests against police abuse erupted on the streets of Kenosha. On August 25, 2020, an administrator of the Kenosha Guard Facebook group posted this message: "Any patriots willing to take up arms and defend [our] City tonight from the evil thugs? No doubt they are currently planning on the next part of the City to burn tonight!"[34]

That night, Rittenhouse took a rifle from his home and traveled the 21 miles (33.8 km) from Antioch to Kenosha, where he patrolled the streets. That same night two protesters were fatally shot in Kenosha. A day later Rittenhouse was charged with the murders. By the fall of 2021, Rittenhouse remained in custody awaiting trial.

As the cases involving Welch and Rittenhouse illustrate, many people believe these baseless conspiracy theories are true. In 2020 a poll commissioned by National Public Radio asked respondents whether they believe QAnon theories. Seventeen percent of respondents said they believed the theories, while another 37 percent said they were not sure, meaning that more than half of the respondents who participated in the poll gave QAnon's conspiracy theories at least some measure of credibility. "It's total bonkers," says Chris Jackson, who headed the polling team that conducted the survey, "and yet . . . essentially half of Americans believe it's true or think that maybe it's true. They don't

> "Any patriots willing to take up arms and defend [our] City tonight from the evil thugs?"[34]
>
> —Kenosha Guard Facebook posting

> "It's total bonkers and yet . . . essentially half of Americans believe it's true or think that maybe it's true."[35]
>
> —Pollster Chris Jackson

Social Media Postings as Evidence

Extremists may use social media to recruit members, spread conspiracy theories, and even plan violent acts, but relying on social media may also have a downside for them. Law enforcement agencies can gain easy access to social media postings, meaning the words of extremists can often be employed as evidence in charging them with crimes.

Indeed, in the weeks following the January 2021 riot at the US Capitol, FBI agents and other law enforcement agencies culled through the social media posts by the rioters. And it did not take them long to find evidence linking extremists with social media accounts to their activities in the Capitol insurrection.

For example, Jenny Cudd, one of the insurgents who allegedly broke into the office of House Speaker Nancy Pelosi, had this to say on her Facebook page: "We just pushed, pushed, and pushed, and yelled go and yelled charge. We just pushed and pushed, and we got in. We did break down Nancy Pelosi's office door." Cudd also posted a live video on Facebook of her activities in the Capitol as the insurrection was unfolding. Assisted in no small measure by the evidence Cudd provided on her own to her Facebook page, a week after the Capitol riot the FBI announced that Cudd, a resident of Midland, Texas, had been arrested by federal agents.

Quoted in Kevin Collier, "Selfies, Social Media Posts Making It Easier for FBI to Track Down Capitol Riot Suspects," NBC News, January 16, 2021. www.nbcnews.com.

really know. And I think that's terrifying that half of Americans believe that could be the case."[35]

Harrison Hawkins's girlfriend is a believer. After meeting on a dating app, Hawkins and his girlfriend grew close. But after a few months, he found her constantly staring at her phone, where she read social media posts that had been created by QAnon—many focusing on conspiracy theories about the COVID-19 pandemic. One theory she mentioned to Hawkins was QAnon's belief that drugs formulated to battle the disease were concocted from the blood of children. Over a period of several months, Hawkins could see her growing more and more anxious as she expressed fears about the future. Now Hawkins does not know if his relationship with his girlfriend can be repaired. "Some media outlets have written [QAnon] off as a kooky conspiracy," he says. "The word 'conspiracy' discredits its power."[36]

Spreading Extremism Before the Internet

The fact that a significant number of people believe the conspiracy theories helps explain how the theories become so widely spread. Indeed, people who believe the theories often assist in spreading them by reposting the theories on their own social media pages. Therefore, the theories are spread quickly and sometimes seen by millions of people—long before experts have the opportunity to debunk the theories.

The spreading of conspiracy theories is not a recent tactic that has been employed by the extremist movement. Kathryn Olmstead, a history professor at the University of California, Davis, points to the rise in conspiracy theories following the assassination of President John F. Kennedy in 1963. Kennedy was shot in Dallas, Texas, while riding in a motorcade. The assassin was a local man, Lee Harvey Oswald. A congressional investigation into the assassination later established that Oswald acted alone. Nevertheless, conspiracy theories soon circulated following Kennedy's murder, suggesting that Oswald was part of a widespread plan to bring down the US government.

These theories were further fed when Oswald himself was murdered shortly after his arrest. He was shot by Jack Ruby, a local nightclub owner, while being led through the basement of the Dallas Police Department. Speculation among extremists focused on the notion that Ruby shot Oswald to make sure he kept silent about the plot. No evidence ever surfaced to suggest that either Oswald or Ruby were part of a wide-scale conspiracy to overthrow the American government. During his trial Ruby said his decision to shoot Oswald was driven by an intense grief he felt after Kennedy's assassination. Ruby was convicted in Oswald's murder and sentenced to death; the conviction was eventually overturned on appeal, but Ruby died of cancer in 1967 before he could be retried for the crime.

Still, extremists aired numerous theories suggesting Ruby and Oswald were coconspirators in a wider plot. Among the extremist groups that spread this theory was the John Birch Society, an ar-

Conspiracy theories are not a new phenomenon. President John F. Kennedy was assassinated in 1963 during a presidential parade through Dallas, Texas. Conspiracy theories about his death have circulated for years.

dently conservative group that blamed the assassination on a Communist plot to overthrow the US government. (This theory was fed by the fact that Oswald had briefly lived in the former Soviet Union, returning to the United States two years before he shot Kennedy.) In this pre-internet age, the "Birchers" and other extremists had few methods to spread their ideas about the Kennedy assassination or to find others in agreement with their theories. "They had to work pretty hard to identify each other," Olmstead says. "They would put up flyers at the local library, or they'd write letters to the editor. And eventually, they had groups and newsletters and they would have conferences. I mean, they did it, but it took a while."[37]

The internet and the establishment of social media platforms have made it far easier for extremist groups to air their messages and recruit followers. Social media has provided a vast resource for extremists to spread their messages and find others who share their worldviews. And all of this happens with little more than a mouse click.

What Drives People Toward Extremism?

The RAND Corporation, a public policy research organization based in Santa Monica, California, has looked into what drives people to join extremist groups. Researchers contacted thirty-two former members of extremist groups and found that in twenty-two cases the members were driven by financial hardship. Facing debt, unemployment, and poverty they searched for someone to blame for their woes. Ultimately, they focused their anger on Blacks, Latinos, Jews, gay Americans, and others. Moreover, in seventeen cases, the RAND researchers determined the former extremists had been suffering mental health issues, such as anxiety or depression, which helped cloud their thinking, drawing them into extremism.

In speaking with the former extremists, the RAND researchers found that the extremists joined groups because they found others who shared their ideas, were sympathetic to their plights, and provided emotional support. Said the RAND study, "Interviewees described how they were motivated to join a group by the social bonds they experienced within the group. Most noted feelings of family and friendship among group members, and some discussed how they felt a new sense of power as a member of a group. Some noted how they felt rewarded for contributions to the cause and group."

Ryan Andrew Brown et al., "What Do Former Extremists and Their Families Say About Radicalization and Deradicalization in America?," RAND Corporation, 2021. www.rand.org.

Extremist Growth Tied to the Internet

The ease and speed of communication and the unprecedented reach of social media have fueled the growth of extremism in America. Although it is difficult to provide estimates of the actual number of Americans who harbor extremist views, some civil rights groups have nevertheless been able to chart the growth of extremism, linking that growth directly to the internet. A 2019 report by the SPLC found the existence of 954 active domestic extremist groups in 2017; in 2018 the SPLC reported that the number had grown to 1,020. And the influence of the internet can perhaps be seen in the growth of these groups. The SPLC report pointed out that in 1999—a time when the internet was still developing and social media was virtually nonexistent—a total of 457 extremist groups were known to exist in the United States.

The SPLC report points to the growth of an extremist group known as Atomwaffen Division to illustrate how extremist groups make use of the internet. Atomwaffen Division is composed of members who advocate for the racist and anti-Semitic principles that propelled the Nazis to power in 1930s Germany. Says the SPLC report:

> [Atomwaffen Division] is very backward-looking, positively nostalgic for the terroristic brands of neo-Nazism promoted by white supremacists from years gone by. Atomwaffen Division is proof that such ideologies continue to prevail . . . Central to the group's action plan is the belief, drawn from these older sources, that the old, established version of Western civilization has to be destroyed utterly and rebuilt entirely free of Jewish and nonwhite influences, reinstituting the totalizing order of [Nazism].
>
> This violent and vicious ideology is almost entirely enabled by the Internet and its ability to connect people with fringe ideologies across large distances. Atomwaffen claims it has about 20 cells scattered around the US, with membership in each cell estimated between three and five people each. That means the group may have about 80 members altogether nationally.[38]

Experts say there is no doubt that social media and the internet have been instrumental in enabling extremist groups to grow, spread their bizarre conspiracy theories, and even plan their violent acts. And sadly, many extremists naively believe what they read on social media. This attitude has caused Harrison Hawkins to lose his relationship with his girlfriend. It caused Edgar M. Welch to blast rifle shots into a pizza restaurant, endangering the diners and staff members inside. And it caused seventeen-year-old Kyle Rittenhouse to take a gun to a protest march and allegedly murder two innocent people.

CHAPTER FOUR

Countering Domestic Extremism

During the riot at the US Capitol, Fi Duong, a resident of Alexandria, Virginia, made his way onto the Capitol grounds. After the demonstrators broke through the doors, Duong entered the building. He took selfies as he wandered throughout the Capitol but, according to law enforcement officials, committed no acts of vandalism in the building nor participated in any of the assaults that occurred during the day.

Duong was not among the extremists who were arrested in the weeks after the January 6 insurrection. Rather, FBI agents believed Duong was involved in far more serious plans and elected to investigate him further. An undercover FBI agent learned that Duong had formed his own extremist group that was meeting regularly in his Alexandria home.

The undercover agent started attending the meetings. At first, according to the FBI, Duong and the others in the unnamed group discussed the Bible and its lessons. But after the Bible study session, the group members discussed far different matters: bomb making, assault tactics, and their plans to form an "autonomous" region of Virginia that would not have to comply with the laws of the state. Duong and his fellow extremists seemed most perturbed at what they regarded as harsh measures imposed by the state government to restrict their rights to own guns. In June 2021 Duong led the members to a remote location in Virginia to surveil the area as a possible site for testing the group's homemade bombs.

According to FBI agents, Duong predicted that his group's coming violent acts would prompt a widespread revolution against the government of Virginia, and he warned the members to be prepared for the chaos that would surely follow. "We're not at a point where people are out in the street rioting," Duong is alleged to have told the group members during that trip. "It's coming soon. I'd give it about another six weeks. . . . Whatever supplies you can get now, get 'em now."[39]

In July 2021 the FBI arrested Duong, charging him only with illegally entering the Capitol on January 6. He was released on bail to await trial. Although federal prosecutors did not lodge charges against him for his alleged intentions to build bombs or use them against the government of Virginia, prosecutors said Duong "repeatedly expressed his willingness to engage in conflict, including violence, against groups that shared different views than his own."[40]

Focusing on Domestic Terrorism

The investigation into Duong illustrates that rooting out extremists and stifling their plans to commit violent acts remains a challenge for law enforcement officials. But officials believe it is a challenge that can be accomplished—that the resources of federal, state, and local law enforcement agencies can be utilized to expose extremists' plans and stifle them before harm is inflicted.

The FBI has focused on domestic terrorism since 1980, when the agency created the Joint Terrorism Task Force. The task force is charged with investigating acts of terrorism planned by foreign and domestic extremists. As the Duong case demonstrates, one method the FBI uses to quash the plans of extremists is to infiltrate their groups with undercover agents. These agents pose as extremists and gain the trust of the leaders while reporting their activities to the agency and in many cases using hidden microphones to record their conversations with group members. These recordings are typically used as evidence against the extremists in court.

In June 2021 US attorney general Merrick Garland spoke about the Justice Department's new strategy for countering domestic extremism. The strategy calls for greater sharing of intelligence, closer monitoring of social media activity of extremists, and more money to support these and other efforts.

US leaders believe more needs to be done. On President Joe Biden's second day in office, he authorized a team of national security advisers to make recommendations on how the federal government should address domestic extremism. Six months later, the team issued its report, titled the *National Strategy for Countering Domestic Terrorism*. The report called on the FBI and other federal law enforcement agencies to work more closely with state and local police agencies, sharing intelligence on extremist activities. Also, the report said law enforcement agencies need to better monitor social media platforms as a way of developing intelligence on extremists' plans. And the report urged Congress to provide $100 million in funding to the FBI and to US Department of Justice prosecutors to better equip them to recognize and react to extremist plans. Says the report:

These efforts speak to a broader priority: enhancing faith in government and addressing the extreme polarization, fueled by a crisis of disinformation and misinformation often channeled through social media platforms, which can tear Americans apart and lead some to violence. A hallmark of this democracy is that political change must be pursued through nonviolent means grounded in the principles upon which the United States was founded. Enhancing faith in American democracy demands accelerating work to contend with an information environment that challenges healthy democratic discourse. We will work toward finding ways to counter the influence and impact of dangerous conspiracy theories that can provide a gateway to terrorist violence.[41]

First Amendment Rights

Increased resources and monitoring by law enforcement agencies are important steps in reversing inroads made by domestic extremists, but these efforts alone cannot reduce the extremist threat. Many experts have called on social media companies to take action against the posting of disinformation, conspiracy theories, and extremist ideologies on their platforms. For years, Facebook, Twitter, Instagram, and other social media platforms did little to monitor or block incendiary extremist content.

Administrators of the major social media platforms were often hesitant to act against these posts, believing such messages and information enjoyed protection under the First Amendment to the US Constitution. The First Amendment, part of the Bill of Rights that was added to the Constitution in 1791, states that free speech is a right enjoyed by all Americans. Administrators of the social media platforms concluded that although posts by extremists may have been racist or otherwise unsavory, under the First Amendment the posters nevertheless had the right to air their views.

But that attitude started changing in 2018 when a group of Proud Boys assaulted protesters who assembled outside a ven-

Many people cringe as they read the hateful words of extremists on social media and elsewhere, but a major American civil rights group insists that extremists—like all others—have the right to express their ideas. For decades, the American Civil Liberties Union (ACLU) has been a staunch defender of the First Amendment right to free speech.

Over the years, the ACLU has provided legal assistance to individuals and groups that believe their First Amendment rights have been denied. In 1979 the ACLU won a court order permitting a neo-Nazi group to march through the streets of Skokie, Illinois, a Chicago suburb known to have a large Jewish population. In a position paper issued in 2021, the ACLU reviewed its position on free speech. This review was prompted by the 2018 White nationalist rally in Charlottesville, Virginia, that led to the death of a counterprotester. The organization examined whether it could still justify defending free speech rights for extremists. Although the ACLU does not condone violence, it declared its policy had not changed—that the extremists had the right to march through Charlottesville and that if called on, the ACLU would again go to court on behalf of extremists to defend their First Amendment rights.

ue in New York City where Proud Boys founder Gavin McInnes was giving a speech. Social media administrators concluded that the assault was sparked by incendiary language posted on the platforms by Proud Boys leaders. Following the assaults on the demonstrators in New York, administrators of Facebook and other popular social media platforms banned posts by extremist groups.

Nevertheless, administrators of social media pages have found that they cannot wipe all extremist rhetoric from their pages. Although organized groups such as the Proud Boys and Oath Keepers have been banned from the major social media platforms, individuals can certainly maintain their own pages. And they often use those pages to post their own fiery and racist rhetoric.

Messaging Apps

Now banned from Facebook, Twitter, Instagram, and other prominent social media platforms, extremist groups have had to find other ways to communicate with followers and potential followers. Some of these groups have created their own websites. For example, the Proud Boys did this, but the group's website was banned in 2020 by its web-hosting service. The ban followed protests by Color of Change, an Oakland, California, civil rights group that demanded the group's site be removed because of its racist content. Other extremist groups have also been rejected by web-hosting services.

Such actions have forced extremist groups to search for alternatives. Many have found those alternatives in messaging apps and imageboards. Messaging apps enable users to engage in real-time online chats. Imageboards enable users to post images. Messaging apps that have become popular with extremist groups include Parler, Rumble, Gab, and Telegram. "As tech companies continue to try to clean up their platforms, other sites have popped up to pick up the 'deplatformed,'" says a report by the SPLC. "Gab is the largest of these alternative sites, with about 800,000 members and 5 million page views a month. The site has very loose terms of service and is home to countless neo-Nazis

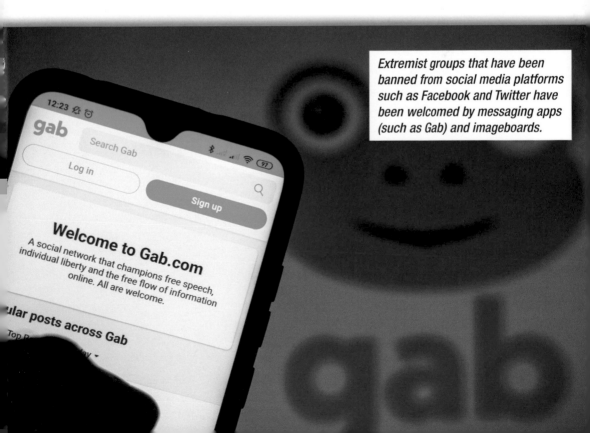

Extremist groups that have been banned from social media platforms such as Facebook and Twitter have been welcomed by messaging apps (such as Gab) and imageboards.

and other extremists."[42] Imageboards that are frequently used by extremists include 8kun and 4chan. These messaging apps and imageboards enable members to post messages and images that can be seen by anyone with internet access.

An additional benefit of these apps is privacy. They enable users to access private channels, where members can carry on exchanges seen only by the participants. Says Kevin Grisham, professor of global studies at California State University, San Bernardino:

> Encrypted messaging platforms like Telegram, which was launched in 2013, have become places for violent extremists to meet up and organize. Telegram serves a dual purpose. It created a space where conversations can occur openly in the service's public channels. Those who wanted more privacy can message one another through private chats.
>
> In these private chats, violent extremists can share tactics, organize themselves and radicalize, something I've observed in my research of hate and extremism. New Telegram users are exposed to violent extremist beliefs on the public side of Telegram and then group members carry out the logistics of recruiting and organizing in the private chats.[43]

The tech companies that provide the messaging apps are frequently located outside the United States. This means they are largely shielded from demands by civil rights groups to bar extremists from their platforms. For example, according to Grisham, the platform used by Parler is provided by a company based in Russia.

"In these private chats, violent extremists can share tactics, organize themselves and radicalize, something I've observed in my research of hate and extremism."[43]

—Kevin Grisham, professor of global studies at California State University, San Bernardino

The US Department of Defense announced plans in 2021 to strengthen its background checks for individuals who seek to join the military. Under the new policy, recruitment officers for the army, navy, air force, and marines will cull through social media postings by potential recruits to see whether they have exhibited extremist behavior. "That could be anything from liking a comment on a social media post that's buried somewhere on the Internet, all the way through openly advocating violence against the government or a government official," says Anthony Kuhn, an attorney who specializes in security clearance issues.

Meanwhile, law enforcement agencies are also striving to eliminate extremists from their ranks. Following the Capitol riot, legislators in several states proposed laws enabling police departments to do more thorough background checks of applicants. But even before adoption of these laws, some city police departments took action on their own. In Fresno, California, for example, a police officer was fired after video surfaced on social media showing him encouraging members of the Proud Boys to participate in a public protest. "Such ideology, behavior and affiliations have no place in law enforcement and will not be tolerated within the ranks of the Fresno Police Department," says Fresno police chief Paco Balderrama.

Quoted in Stephen Losey, "Pentagon Eyes Plan to Intensify Social Media Screening in Military Background Investigations," Military.com, May 3, 2021. www.military.com.

Quoted in Neil MacFarquhar, "Efforts to Weed Out Extremists in Law Enforcement Meet Resistance," *New York Times*, May 11, 2021. www.nytimes.com.

Recognizing the Growth of Extremism

While technology companies try to scrub extremist messages from their social media platforms, other efforts are underway to curb extremist conduct. Two weeks after the Capitol riot, members of Congress introduced versions of the proposed Domestic Terrorism Prevention Act of 2021 in the House and Senate. Among the provisions of the proposed law is the requirement that all law enforcement officers undergo training to help them recognize extremism and how it may be evolving in the communities they police. Moreover, the law would require the FBI to issue reports every six months on the growth of domestic extremism. This would include identifying specific communities where extremism appears to be growing.

This provision would authorize the police to use their powers of surveillance to keep watch on and, if needed, infiltrate extremist groups. According to a news release issued by the US Senate Judiciary Committee, the proposed law would require law enforcement to "assess the domestic terrorism threat posed by white supremacists [and] analyze domestic terrorism incidents that occurred in the previous six months."[44] Moreover, the proposed law requires law enforcement agencies to share information that would help them determine whether national extremist movements are forming—trends they might ordinarily miss if they are focused only on local developments.

By the fall of 2021, Congress had yet to act on the proposed law. Critics warned that the law could deprive people of their legitimate First Amendment rights to free speech. Brian Michael Jenkins, a former US Army captain and an author who studies issues involving terrorism, is among those who believe the law goes too far. He suggests that prosecutors already have the authority to bring cases against extremists who plan or commit acts of violence.

Jenkins cites a 2021 University of Chicago study that found just 10 percent of the participants in the Capitol insurrection were members of organized extremist groups, such as the Proud Boys and Oath Keepers. According to the study, most everyone else who showed up at the Capitol that morning were individuals who truly believed the election had been stolen and wanted to exercise their First Amendment rights to protest. Of the thousands of protesters who gathered at the Capitol, about six hundred violated the law by breaking into the Capitol; the rest remained outside and broke no laws. Says Jenkins:

> About 10 percent of the invaders of the Capitol were members of known extremist groups—they came to fight. About 90 percent were ordinary people who believed that they were taking patriotic action to prevent the election from being stolen. They were wrong, but there is a risk of tarring a significant slice of the country as affiliating with

terrorists . . . the goal in dealing with domestic violent extremists is to isolate them from potential constituencies, not broaden the target.[45]

Accepting Societal Change

Jenkins and other experts believe that rather than empowering the government with new authority to root out extremist activity, the key to wiping out extremism is to reach out to the individuals who joined the movement and convince them that they should be more willing to accept American culture as it continues to evolve. Christian Picciolini left the extremist movement in 1996. By then he had opened a music store in Chicago and found that many of his customers—Blacks, Latinos, Jews, and others whom he had grown to hate—were in fact friendly, ordinary people who meant him no harm. He found himself questioning his extremist ideology and decided there was no truth in the conspiracy theories he had

At a 2017 event Christian Picciolini talks about what drove him into the White supremacist movement and how he found his way out of it. Picciolini founded the Free Radicals Project, a global extremism prevention and education network.

come to believe. Since leaving the extremist movement, Picciolini has founded the Free Radicals Project, which works to educate extremists on the values of inclusion and acceptance of societal change.

In many cases, Picciolini says, extremists embrace their radical ideologies because something has gone wrong in their own lives. Perhaps they had difficult childhoods that included physical violence or abuse. Perhaps they have substance abuse problems, making it difficult to maintain relationships or hold down a job. Rather than look inward to recognize their own faults, he says, extremists often look to blame others and invariably focus on racist notions. Picciolini says his organization works with individuals to recognize that their problems are not the result of a changing culture around them, but rather they face individual issues that have stifled their own personal growth. "Over time, with space for self-reflection, hatred for others often reveals itself as the projection of gaping deficits for love or respect for oneself," he says. "It amazes me every time I see the crutches of hate jettisoned and watch prejudice melt away, all without aggressively confronting someone about their nasty beliefs."[46]

> "It amazes me every time I see the crutches of hate jettisoned and watch prejudice melt away, all without aggressively confronting someone about their nasty beliefs."[46]
>
> —Former extremist leader Christian Picciolini

Picciolini's experience illustrates that it is possible for extremists to reform themselves—to accept change and regard others as equals. It may be a slow process and might not always succeed, but domestic extremism poses threats that must be addressed. The Capitol riot of January 2021 was a sort of wake-up call that highlighted the growing problem of domestic extremism. Various strategies will likely be needed and are being tried to confront this threat and to ensure that positive cultural change remains a part of life in America for now and the future.

SOURCE NOTES

Introduction: The Wolverine Watchmen

1. Quoted in Gus Burns, "13 Men Face Charges in Plot to Kidnap Michigan Gov. Gretchen Whitmer, Start 'Civil War,'" MLive.com, October 9, 2020. www.mlive.com.
2. Quote in Anabel Sosa, "Who Are the Wolverine Watchmen, the Group Allegedly Part of Thwarted Plan to Kidnap Michigan Governor?," *Inside Edition*, October 14, 2020. www.insideedition.com.

Chapter One: The Threat Posed by Domestic Extremism

3. Quoted in Adeel Hassan, "White Supremacist Guilty of Killing 2 Who Came to Aid of Black Teens," *New York Times*, July 23, 2020. www.nytimes.com.
4. Quoted in CBS News, "Woman Cries Recalling Suspect's Hate-Filled Tirade Before Deadly Portland Train Attack," January 29, 2020. www.cbsnews.com.
5. Quoted in Corey Pein and Nigel Jaquiss, "Who Radicalized Jeremy Christian? Alt-Right Extremists Rush to Distance Themselves from MAX Slaying Suspect," *Portland (OR) Willamette Week*, May 31, 2017. www.wweek.com.
6. Quoted in Shane Dixon Kavanaugh, "Muslim Teen Targeted Before MAX Train Slaying: 'Our Faces Were a Trigger,'" *Oregonian* (Portland, OR), January 29, 2019. www.oregonlive.com.
7. Quoted in Robert O'Harrow Jr. et al., "The Rise of Domestic Terrorism Is Fueled Mostly by Far-Right Extremists, Analysis Shows," *Philadelphia Inquirer*, April 12, 2021. www.inquirer.com.
8. Anti-Defamation League, "Extremism," 2021. www.adl.org.
9. Federal Bureau of Investigation, *Strategic Intelligence Assessment and Data on Domestic Terrorism*, May 2021. www.fbi.gov.
10. Quoted in Associated Press, "Judges Uphold the Death Sentence for Dylann Roof Who Killed 9 Black Churchgoers," National Public Radio, August 25, 2021. www.npr.org.
11. Quoted in Lee Brown, "Neo-Nazi Ex-Soldier Jailed for Bomb Plot to Overthrow Government," *New York Post*, August 20, 2020. https://nypost.com.

12. Quoted in Heidi Beirich, "Rage Against Change," *Southern Poverty Law Center Intelligence Report*, Spring 2019, p. 38. www.splcenter.org.
13. Chris Bosley, "Transforming Domestic Extremism in the United States," Cairo Review of Global Affairs, April 28, 2021. www.thecairoreview.com.
14. Christian Picciolini, *Breaking Hate: Confronting the New Culture of Extremism*. New York: Hachette, 2020, p. xxi.

Chapter Two: The Rise of Extremist Groups

15. Quoted in Natasha Lipman, "Christian Picciolini: The Neo-Nazi Who Became an Anti-Nazi," BBC, December 5, 2020. www.bbc.com.
16. Quoted in Lipman, "Christian Picciolini."
17. Quoted in Lipman, "Christian Picciolini."
18. Quoted in Emma Mayer, "'Hitler Was Right': Neo-Nazis Arrive at Pro-Israel Rally in Van Covered with Hate Speech," *Newsweek*, May 13, 2021. www.newsweek.com.
19. Quoted in Mayer, "'Hitler Was Right.'"
20. Quoted in Larry Diffey, "Obama Must Be Impeached and Removed to Stop His 'Amnesty' of Illegals," Oathkeepers.org, November 20, 2014. https://oathkeepers.org.
21. Quoted in Southern Poverty Law Center, "Oath Keepers," 2021. www.splcenter.org.
22. Quoted in Alexandra Hall, "The Proud Boys: Drinking Club or Misogynist Movement?," *To the Best of Our Knowledge*, February 3, 2018. www.ttbook.org.
23. Quoted in Hall, "The Proud Boys."
24. Quoted in Adam G. Klein, "In Trump, Extremism Found Its Champion—and Maybe Its Demise," The Conversation, November 7, 2016. https://theconversation.com.
25. Quoted in Jordyn Phelps, "Trump Defends 2017 'Very Fine People' Comments, Calls Robert E. Lee 'a Great General,'" ABC News, April 26, 2019. https://abcnews.go.com.
26. Quoted in Associated Press, "Transcript of Trump's Speech at Rally Before US Capitol Riot," January 13, 2021. https://apnews.com.
27. Quoted in Masood Farivar, "Researchers: More than a Dozen Extremist Groups Took Part in Capitol Riots," Voice of America News, January 16, 2021. www.voanews.com.

Chapter Three: How Extremists Grow Their Ranks

28. Quoted in Zach Crenshaw, "'Proud Boys' Have Been Recruiting in Arizona for Months," ABC 15, September 30, 2020. www.abc15.com.
29. Quoted in Crenshaw, "'Proud Boys' Have Been Recruiting in Arizona for Months."
30. Quoted in Tucker Higgins, "Alex Jones' 5 Most Disturbing and Ridiculous Conspiracy Theories," CNBC, September 14, 2018. www.cnbc.com.

31. Southern Poverty Law Center, "Tall Tales Spread by Alex Jones Breed Dangerous Plots," 2021. www.splcenter.org.
32. Quoted in Luke Kenton, "Conspiracy Theories About George Soros Organizing and Fueling the Unrest in the US Sparked by the Death of George Floyd Soar Online," *Daily Mail* (London), June 21, 2020. www.dailymail.co.uk.
33. Talia Lavin, *Culture Warlords: My Journey Into the Dark Web of White Supremacy*. New York: Hachette, 2020, p. 21.
34. Quoted in Dan Mihalopoulos, "Kenosha Shooting Suspect Fervently Supported 'Blue Lives,' Joined Local Militia," National Public Radio, August 27, 2020. www.npr.org.
35. Quoted in Joel Rose, "Even If It's 'Bonkers,' Poll Finds Many Believe QAnon and Other Conspiracy Theories," National Public Radio, December 30, 2020. www.npr.org.
36. Quoted in Nathan Bomey and Jessica Guynn, "How QAnon and Other Dark Forces Are Radicalizing Americans as the COVID-19 Pandemic Rages and Election Looms," *USA Today*, October 2, 2020. www.usatoday.com.
37. Quoted in Joel Rose, "'More Dangerous and More Widespread': Conspiracy Theories Spread Faster than Ever," National Public Radio, March 2, 2021. www.npr.org.
38. David Neiwert, "Violent Nostalgia," *Southern Poverty Law Center Intelligence Report*, Spring 2019, pp. 10–11. www.splcenter.org.

Chapter Four: Countering Domestic Extremism

39. Quoted in Hannah Rabinowitz and Katelyn Polantz, "FBI Infiltrates Group That Wanted to Test Bombs, Surveil Capitol, Secede from US, Court Records Show," WESH 2, July 7, 2021. www.wesh.com.
40. Quoted in Jordan Fischer et al., "Alexandria Man Talked of Shootout with Feds After Capitol Riot, FBI Says," WUSA 9, July 6, 2021. www.wusa9.com.
41. National Security Council, *National Strategy for Countering Domestic Terrorism*. Washington, DC: National Security Council, June 2021, p. 29. www.whitehouse.gov.
42. Beirich, "Rage Against Change."
43. Kevin Grisham, "Far-Right Groups Move to Messaging Apps as Tech Companies Crack Down on Extremist Social Media," The Conversation, January 22, 2021. https://theconversation.com.
44. US Senate Judiciary Committee, "Durbin Reintroduces Legislation to Combat Rising Domestic Terrorist Threat," March 25, 2021. www.judiciary.senate.gov.
45. Brian Michael Jenkins, "Five Reasons to Be Wary of a New Domestic Terrorism Law," *The RAND Blog*, RAND Corporation, February 24, 2021. www.rand.org.
46. Picciolini, *Breaking Hate*, p. 136.

Anti-Defamation League (ADL)

www.adl.org

The ADL fights anti-Semitism, extremism, and hate. By accessing the Research & Tools tab on the ADL website, visitors can find the group's interactive Hate, Extremism, Anti-Semitism and Terrorism (HEAT) map. By using the map, visitors can learn the details of some eight thousand extremist incidents in the United States.

Domestic Terrorism, RAND Corporation

www.rand.org/topics/domestic-terrorism.html

This public policy research organization has devoted this website to an analysis of domestic terrorism in America. Articles and videos on the site explore issues such as extremism in the US military, how former extremists found new lives after leaving the movement, and how social media serves as a platform for extremist views.

Free Radicals Project (FRP)

www.freeradicals.org

Established by former extremist Christian Picciolini, the FRP works with law enforcement agencies to help give them insight into how extremist groups organize and operate. The FRP also works with individuals as it strives to convince them to give up extremism and become more accepting of change and inclusion.

Issues: Conspiracy Theories, FactCheck.org

www.factcheck.org/issue/conspiracy-theories

FactCheck.org, which was established by the University of Pennsylvania, is devoted to analyzing comments made in the media by political figures to determine whether they are telling the truth. The organization has devoted this site to debunking the various conspiracy theories that are posted on social media platforms.

Southern Poverty Law Center (SPLC)
www.splcenter.org
The Montgomery, Alabama–based group monitors extremist activity in America. By accessing the link for Extremist Files on the group's website, visitors can find profiles of groups and individuals who harbor extremist ideologies. Among the profiles that are listed are those for the Proud Boys, Oath Keepers, and Ku Klux Klan.

U.S. Capitol Violence, Federal Bureau of Investigation (FBI)
www.fbi.gov/wanted/capitol-violence
Maintained by the FBI, this website is devoted to the bureau's investigation into the January 6, 2021, riot at the US Capitol. Visitors can find several videos that were obtained from social media posts by participants in the riot. The FBI is seeking information on rioters who can be seen in the videos but have not yet been identified.

Books

J.M. Berger, *Extremism*. Cambridge, MA: MIT Press, 2018.

Robert M. Henderson, *The Spread of Hate and Extremism*. San Diego, CA: ReferencePoint, 2021.

Michael Kimmel, *Healing from Hate: How Young Men Get into—and out of—Violent Extremism*. Oakland: University of California Press, 2018.

Talia Lavin, *Culture Warlords: My Journey into the Dark Web of White Supremacy*. New York: Hachette, 2020.

Christian Picciolini, *Breaking Hate: Confronting the New Culture of Extremism*. New York: Hachette, 2020.

Joseph E. Uscinski, *Conspiracy Theories: A Primer*. New York: Rowman & Littlefield, 2020.

Internet Sources

Masood Farivar, "Researchers: More than a Dozen Extremist Groups Took Part in Capitol Riots," Voice of America News, January 16, 2021. www.voanews.com.

Kevin Grisham, "Far-Right Groups Move to Messaging Apps as Tech Companies Crack Down on Extremist Social Media," The Conversation, January 22, 2021. https://theconversation.com.

Natasha Lipman, "Christian Picciolini: The Neo-Nazi Who Became an Anti-Nazi," BBC, December 5, 2020. www.bbc.com.

Joel Rose, "Even If It's 'Bonkers,' Poll Finds Many Believe QAnon and Other Conspiracy Theories," National Public Radio, December 30, 2020. www.npr.org.

Anabel Sosa, "Who Are the Wolverine Watchmen, the Group Allegedly Part of Thwarted Plan to Kidnap Michigan Governor?," *Inside Edition*, October 14, 2020. www.insideedition.com.

INDEX

Note: Boldface page numbers indicate illustrations.

Alfred P. Murrah Federal Building (Oklahoma City), 14, **14**
alt-right movement, 12, 17–18
American Civil Liberties Union (ACLU), 48
Anti-Defamation League (ADL), 12, 24, 37, 58
anti-Semitism, 23–24, 36–37
Atomwaffen Division (German extremist group), 43

Balderrama, Paco, 51
Bannon, Steve, 28–29
Beda, Steven, 17
Best, Rick, 11
Biden, Joe, 46
Black Lives Matter (BLM) movement, 19
Boogaloo Bois, 23, 31
Bosley, Chris, 19, 20
Breitbart News (website), 28–29
Brooks, Samantha Frances, 17

California Patriots Pro Law & Order, 35
Center for Strategic & International Studies (CSIS), 13, 16
Charleston church shooting (SC, 2015), 15
Charlottesville White supremacist march (VA, 2017), 15, **18**, 30
Chicago Area Skinheads (CASH), 22
Christian, Jeremy, 10–11

Clinton, Hillary, 27
conspiracy theories
  belief in, 37–39
  "Pizzagate," 34–35
  predating internet, 40–41
  QAnon and, 33, **34**
  social media and spread of, 35–37
COVID-19 pandemic
  conspiracy theories and, 39
  protests against responses to, 6, 8, 9
Crabtree, Daniel, 16
Cudd, Jenny, 39

Davey, Jacob, 25
Deferred Action for Childhood Arrivals (DACA), 26
Department of Defense, US, 51
domestic extremism
  FBI task force on, 45
  important events in history of, **4–5**
  White House report on, 46–47
domestic terrorism, 13–15
  definition of, 13
Domestic Terrorism, RAND Corporation (website), 58
Domestic Terrorism Prevention Act (proposed, 2021), 51–52
Duong, Fi, 44–45

Ebner, Julia, 25
eco-terrorism, 17
Equal Justice Initiative, 25
extremism/extremist groups
  definition of, 12
  motivations for joining, 42, 54

numbers of, 42
in police/military, 16–17
as response to societal change,
   17–20
women and, 25, 27–28

Facebook, 8, 16, 38
   banning of extremist groups on, 48
   QAnon conspiracy theories
      circulated on, 35
   racist officers exposed by posts
      on, 17
Federal Bureau of Investigation (FBI),
   7, 13, 31, 45
   U.S. Capitol Violence website, 59
Fields, James Alex, Jr., 15
First Amendment, 47, 48
Fletcher, Micah David-Cole, 11
Floyd, George, 19, 35, **36**
Free Radicals Project (FRP), 54, 58

Gab (messaging app), **49**, 49–50
Garbin, Ty, 9
Garland, Merrick, **46**
Goyim Defense League (GDL), 24
Grisham, Kevin, 50

Hawkins, Harrison, 39, 43
Heyer, Heather, 15, 30
Hitler, Adolf, 23–24
Holzer, Richard, 13–14

ideologies, of perpetrators of
   extremist attacks/plots, **13**
imageboards, 49, 50
immigration
   alt-right movement and, 12
   hostility toward, 26
   Trump and, 27
Ingraham, Laura, 18
Institute for Strategic Dialogue, 35
Issues: Conspiracy Theories,
   FactCheck.org, 58

Jackson, Chris, 38–39

January 6 insurrection (Washington,
   DC, 2021), **30**, 30–31
   FBI website devoted to, 59
   social media postings as evidence
      in, 39
Jenkins, Brian Michael, 52, 53
John Birch Society, 40–41
Joint Terrorism Task Force (FBI), 45
Jones, Alex, 33–35
Jones, Seth, 9, 12

Kennedy, John F., 40, **41**
Kenosha Guard, 38
Kuhn, Anthony, 51
Ku Klux Klan, 24–26

LaRosa, Tara, 25
Lavin, Talia, 37
law enforcement/police, extremism
   in, 16–17, 51
liberals, 12
lynchings, 24–25

Magnum, Destinee, 10
Martell, Clark, 22
Mason, Christopher, 29
McInnes, Gavin, 28, 48
McVeigh, Timothy, 14–15
messaging apps, 49–50
military, extremism in, 16–17, 51
misogyny, 25
Mohamed, Walia, 10, 11
Morrison, Joe, 7–9
Mother Emanuel AME Church, 15

Namkai-Meche, Taliesin Myrddin,
   10–11
*National Strategy for Countering
   Domestic Terrorism* (National
   Security Council), 46–47
Nessel, Dana, 7
Nextdoor (social media platform), 32

Oath Keepers, 23, 26, 31
   banning of, on social media, 48

Obama, Barack, 26–27
Office of National Intelligence, US, 19
Oklahoma City bombing (1995), 14,
    14
Olmstead, Kathryn, 40, 41
Oswald, Lee Harvey, 40–41

Pelosi, Nancy, 39
Picciolini, Christian, 20, 21–23, 53,
    53
"Pizzagate" conspiracy theory, 34
police. *See* law enforcement/police
Proud Boys, 23, **23**, 31, 47–48, 51
    banning of, on social media, 48
    recruitment efforts on social media,
        32–33

QAnon, 33, **34**, 35
    opinion on, 38

RAND Corporation, 42, 58
Reiche, Ellen Brennan, 17
Rhodes, Stewart, 26, 27
Rise of the Moors, 29
Rittenhouse, Kyle, 38
Roof, Dylann, 15
Ruby, Jack, 40

Sherwin, Michael, 31
Smith, Jarrett William, 16
social media, 25
    alternatives to, 48–50
    conspiracy theories spread on,
        35–37
    extremist recruitment efforts on,
        32–33
    free speech rights *vs.* extremism
        on, 47–48
societal change
    extremism as reaction to, 17–20
    teaching acceptance of, 53–54

Soros, George, 35–37
Southern Poverty Law Center
    (SPLC), 26, 29, 31, 42, 59
sovereign citizens groups, 29
survey, on belief in QAnon theories,
    38

terrorist plots/attacks
    to kidnap Michigan governor, 6–7,
        8–9
    linked to extremist movements,
        prevalence of, 11–12
    perpetrators of, by ideology, **13**
Third Reich, 11
Thirteenth Amendment, 24
Trump, Donald, 27, 28, 29–30
    January 6 insurrection and, 30
    supporters of, **34**

Unite the Right rally (Charlottesville,
    VA, 2017), 15, **18**, 30

Valle, Jovanni, 24

Washington Post (newspaper),
    11–12, 19
Weary, Darnesha, 19
Welch, Edgar M., 34–35, 37–38,
    43
White nationalist principles, 12
White nationalists, 11, 15, **18**, 29,
    32, 48
    anti-Semitism and, 37
    ideology of, 12
    women and normalization of, 25
Whitmer, Gretchen, 6–7, **8**
Wilson, Timothy, 16
Wolverine Watchmen, 6–9
women
    in extremist groups, 25
    Proud Boys and, 27–28

PICTURE CREDITS